Eight Steps to Writing Your Memoir

David Cariens

HighTide
Publications, Inc.

Deltaville, Virginia

High Tide Publications, Inc.
1000 Bland Point
Deltaville, Virginia 23043
www.hightidepublications.com

Second Edition (revised)

ISBN: 978-1-945990-23-6

Book Design and Cover: FireBelliedFrog.com (www.FireBelliedFrog.com)

Edited by Cindy Loomis Freeman

Contents

Foreword

I have taught non-fiction, analytic writing for over 30 years. This book is my first step into a new realm of writing—creative non-fiction. It is also the prelude to writing my own memoir, a task that is proving to be more daunting than I had first imagined.

When my publisher, Jeanne Johansen, broached the idea of my writing this textbook, I jumped at the chance. As I said in the Acknowledgments, Jeanne had already done much of the research into the project, and I welcomed the opportunity to build on her excellent spadework. Working on this book also was a perfect way to learn the basics of memoir writing.

A memoir is a wonderful legacy and gift to leave a person's family. So many times I have wished that my parents and grandparents had left a written record of their lives and their experiences. Indeed, my decision to write my own memoir comes from a request from my youngest son for me to write an autobiography. It was in studying the differences between biographies, autobiographies, and a memoir that I learned a memoir was a better vehicle for me.

I hope the publication of this book will encourage others to tell their stories.

Chapter 1

Ah, Memoir! What Exactly are You?

It is confusing. Even Amazon is confused. They lump Autobiography and Memoir together as one giant classification. Of course, Amazon can do as it pleases when classifying books. WE, however, are going to dig a little deeper. While some people use the terms interchangeably, we are not. In this first chapter, we look at the three categories of personal story writing: Biography, Autobiography, and Memoir.

Writing in any form can be intimidating. We know intuitively that when we write, we are exposing many things about ourselves: our knowledge of English, our level of education, and our ability to put together a logical essay. Writing also gives the reader a glimpse into our thought processes.

Because memoir is writing about you, it is often the most difficult type of writing. Unless you have had the "perfect" life, this journey through your memories often opens doors long closed. You are forced to remember uncomfortable issues and events. You will need to make decisions about how, and if, you address them. Many of these recollections have not been confronted or thought about for years. It is your call about how to handle them. In some cases, it may be best to keep the door closed. In others, writing about something painful can be cathartic for you and educational for those who read your words.

You need to be honest when you write. The reader will quickly pick up on dishonesty, or writing that is meant to be self-aggrandizing, or words that are meant to hurt intentionally. So, be not only honest, but be fair. And remember if you cannot be as honest and objective as possible, don't go into a subject, person, or event.

Now that the above is out of the way, we can begin by defining a biography, an autobiography, and a memoir. Then we will better understand what a memoir is and how it differs from the first two. Once we understand the differences between them, we can zero in exclusively on the topic of this book—writing a memoir.

Biography

A biography is a nonfiction story of a person's life and must be as true as possible. Briefly, here are the main characteristics of a biography:

- It is not written by the person whose story is being told.

- It is nonfiction and must be as truthful as possible. It is based on factual evidence and almost always marches through a person's life in chronological order.

- It is detail rich—the nitty-gritty of a person's life.

- It requires a great deal of research versus memory.

Most biographies today are split into two types: popular nonfiction books about celebrities, politicians, historical figures, and academic works based on scholarly research. I should note that many of the popular biographies really need a separate category because often they have more of an artificial or controversial slant, like the new biographies of Malcolm X and Gandhi, which claim that both might have had gay love affairs. The artificiality of these books runs counter to the assertion made in point #2 above about truthfulness.

So, that is the definition of a biography, but that is not what you will be writing. While the memoir should be truthful, it is the story of one aspect of a person's life. It does not have to be presented in chronological order, and usually does not require a great deal of research.

Autobiography

Someone once called an autobiography an "authorbiography." That is accurate if you think about it and may be a better name for it. An autobiography is the author's story as she or he wants it told.

Here are the main characteristics of an autobiography:

Unlike a biography, an autobiography is written by the person whose story is being told.

- It, like a biography, is a nonfiction story about a person's life.

- It does not share the need for factual evidence that a biography requires.

- An autobiography requires some research, but a great deal depends on the writer's memories or diaries.

The autobiography falls into the same trappings and styles of a biography. It tells the story of a life from birth to the present day. Unless you are writing a detailed history of your life in chronological order from the time you were born to now, you are not writing an autobiography.

Memoir

A memoir is narrative nonfiction. It also is creative nonfiction in the sense the author is trying to create a mood and accurately capture the emotions surrounding the story or point(s) being made. Because it is impossible to capture the exact substance of conversations or events that happened ten, twenty, fifty years ago, there must be an element of creativity in a memoir. The trick in being creative is to be as accurate as possible and truthful.

A memoir, then, instead of telling about the entire life of a person, tells only about a certain period, or about a certain story arc of the author's life.

Many memoirs deal with depression, abuse, or drugs, or on the other end of the scale, extraordinary, life-changing events. They can also come from celebrities and famous figures, but these are generally limited to books that are ghostwritten by someone else. These books simply adopt the less formal style of the memoir for mass-market appeal. Memoirs are more individualized in style and tone than biographies and autobiographies, and are less formal. Indeed, they can, and often do, take on a conversational tone.

The memoir writer may manipulate his or her own past to improve the story-either moving events around, merging several people into one, or changing the scene of an event to create a better emotional climax. These are considered valid changes in a memoir, if most the story is not fabricated, as it was in the case of James Frey's *A Million Little Pieces*.

Memoirs can be told in any order. Flashback can be used to recall how past events influence current ones. *The Hero's Journey* method can be used, often in the case of overcoming substance abuse or changing your life's path.

So, if you're writing only about your service in World War II or your days as a Broadway dancer, you're crafting a memoir. If you're starting with your birth and providing your life's details, you are writing an autobiography.

⚔

The story in your memoir tells who you are, what you believe, and where you are on your life's path currently. Everyone has a story. Your story is powerful because your sense of self-worth lives in your storyline. Your thoughts and beliefs are powerful energies that can, and do, shape your emotional responses to past events in your life, and thus have fashioned your story.

Many memoir writers have great stories in certain areas of their lives in which they enjoy some measure of success and happiness, but not in others. The bottom line is, unless you learn to let go of your need for others' approval to feel worthwhile, you will have difficulty in processing emotions such as fear and anger in ways that allow you to write your story without sounding angry or vindictive. So, you should put aside many of your concerns about what people will think and write from the heart. That is not easy to do, because all of us (or almost all of us) have spent our lives concerned about what others will think of us and trying not to offend anyone or group of people.

Eight Principles of Memoir Writing

Here are eight characteristics of memoir writing as described by Judith Barrington in her excellent book, *Writing the Memoir*:

1. In memoir writing, the voice is conversational.

2. A memoir requires the reader feels spoken to.

3. Modern memoirs aim to speak immediately to the reader.

4. In a memoir, the author can (and often does) speak directly to the reader.

5. A memoir can move backward and forward in time, recreate believable dialogue, switch scenes and summary, and control the pace and tension of the story.

6. A memoir is a hybrid between fiction and essay.

7. In a memoir, it is important you select a theme.

8. In memoir writing you will be keeping other material for later. (Most people only write one autobiography, but you may write several memoirs).

Before you begin the first set of exercises, I want to leave you with one thought: A memoir is not the story of your life, rather it is stories about your life.

Exercises for Chapter 1

Brainstorm your life.

Make a list of major events and/or defining moments in your life.

Defining Event	Why?

Pick three of the items on your list. Write a brief essay on each, concentrating on why you selected this event.

Time-line Worksheets

When creating your time-line, you may find it easier to recall memories in random order rather than attempting to list the details in chronological order. Often, as we recall things, we will recall another event. This worksheet will help you list your memories as they occur to you. After you are finished, use the worksheets to create a chronological list by stage and further list them by age.

We consider stages as follows:

Stage 1 Childhood: Birth to 11-12 (The beginning of puberty)

Stage 2 Adolescence: Puberty to age 19

Stage 3 Young Adult: Age 20-29

Stage 4 Adult: Age 30-44

Stage 5 Middle Adult: Age 45-59

Stage 6 Late Adult: Age 60-79

Stage 7 Elder: Age 80 plus

Chronological age is not what moves you from one stage to the next.

What moves you is a sense of aging out of the current stage and moving to the next stage:

a. Life events move you on

b. What you have learned moves you

c. A shifting of personal desires and needs moves you on

Each stage is defined by the specific and unique life tasks and challenges it holds for those passing through it. Many people are amazed at the challenges and opportunities they have had over their lifetime. In the sample chart, you can see the passing from one stage to the next. Often it is a time of turmoil and transition, and the previous stage ends when you start questioning your life in that stage:

- What did you want that you couldn't have in that stage of life?
- Can your life be satisfying in its current stage?
- Where is this stage taking you?

The time-line will help us delve into these memories in the next section. Please duplicate these worsheets to meet your needs. Using the worksheet below, you can put together a time-line. You can also rate the experience as positive (+) or negative (-). I suggest you check off each item from the time-line worksheet as you add it to your time-line.

Stage   Sample Worksheet

1	2	3	4	5	6	7	Age	Event
x							0	I was born on March 30, 1958
x							11	My parents divorced and my dad left
		x					22	My son was born
	x						18	I got married
			x				40	I got divorced and became a single parent
			x				42	My mother died
x							6	We moved from Ontario to Cucamonga
				x			45	I got my masters degree
		x					30	My boss said I had to get a degree in economics or no promotion
			x				34	I started night school and got my degree
		x					22	I moved to Hawaii

Sample Time-line:

Stage	Age	Event	Impact (+/-)
1	0	I was born	+
	6	We moved from Ontario to Cucamonga	-
	11	My parents divorced and my dad left	-
2	18	I got married	+
3	22	My son was born	+
	22	I moved to Hawaii	+
	30	My boss said I had to get a degree in economics or no promotion	-
	34	I went back to night school and got my degree	+
4	40	I got divorced and became a single parent	+
	42	My mother died	-
	45	I got my masters degree	+

Time-line Worksheet

1	2	3	4	5	6	7	Age	Event

Stage 1 Childhood: Birth to 11-12 (The beginning of puberty)
Stage 2 Adolescence: Puberty to age 19   Stage 3 Young Adult: Age 20-29
Stage 4 Adult: Age 30-44   Stage 5 Middle Adult: Age 45-59
Stage 6 Late Adult: Age 60-79   Stage 7 Elder: Age 80 plus

1	2	3	4	5	6	7	Age	Event

Stage 1 Childhood: Birth to 11-12 (The beginning of puberty)
Stage 2 Adolescence: Puberty to age 19   Stage 3 Young Adult: Age 20-29
Stage 4 Adult: Age 30-44   Stage 5 Middle Adult: Age 45-59
Stage 6 Late Adult: Age 60-79   Stage 7 Elder: Age 80 plus

Time-line

Stage	Age	Event	Impact (+/-)

A Time-line of Your Life

Putting your time-line on paper is an opportunity to record vital information about your life and your past. There are several benefits to completing this exercise. It helps you:

- See the themes that connect and cut across seemingly different events.

- Recognize key achievements, growth opportunities, lessons, persons, new wisdom, and so on.

- Realize the value of negative shifts as opportunities toward positive shifts.

- Increase a sense of purpose by connecting life events in new ways.

- Find new meanings for your life at present in relation to your past and future.

- Understand how your experiences better prepared you to face future challenges.

- Note how your responses to events shaped your life and character (not the events themselves).

Steps to Building Your Time-line:

List life events using the following guidelines:

- Include experiences, both positive and negative, that influenced your life and later successes.

- There should be a significant life event every year or every few years.

- Be sure to include negative events or turns, keeping in mind they can be essential, if not more so than the positive ones.

- Put the events in chronological order of your age. A worksheet is available on the following pages.

- Put a "+" sign after the events that are overall positive and a "—" sign after those that are negative.

Stage	Age	Event	Impact (+/-)

Stage	Age	Event	Impact (+/-)

Chapter 2 - Step 1

What I Want People to Know

My father was a contractor in the small community where I grew up. People would say, "Who are you, little girl?" I would say, "I am Gene Smith's daughter."

My mother got tired of hearing me say that. "Just give them your name," she would say. "You don't need to say, 'I am Gene Smith's daughter.' You are your own person; not Gene Smith's daughter."

So, the next time she had a group of women come to the house, one of them asked me who I was. I gave them my name. "Aren't you Gene Smith's daughter," they often asked.

I replied, "My mother says I'm not!"

That is a humorous anecdote, but it speaks volumes about how people see us and pigeonhole us based on family. Or, sometimes people view or judge us based on where we live or what we do for a living. Too often people view us by factors that have no relation to reality.

Now, in writing your memoir, you can set the record straight; you can tell your story. What is the single most important thing you want people to know about you? Write that in five words or less here:

I want people to know that I am_____.

Here are some answers others have given:

- I want people to know that I am a child of God.

- I want people to know that I am a writer.

- I want people to know that I am a recovered addict.

- I want people to know that I once belonged to the KKK.

- I want people to know that I am a warrior.

- I want people to know that I survived breast cancer.

Very different answers, right? This question is important because it is what YOU want others to see in you.

As you start writing your memoir, this "I want people know that I am" statement may change. It often does because, as you begin your journey down memory lane, you begin to see yourself differently. In fact, there is a very good chance that this sentence will change. That has happened to me as I worked on my memoir.

Often, authors find out that what they thought was their life story (their quest) is not THEIR story at all. It might deal with their parent's expectations. It might deal with their spouse's expectations. It might deal with coping with a family member's mental illness, alcoholism, or other problems.

On occasion, an author who is a doctor, will say, "I want people to know I am a physician." But when they start the writing process, that isn't what they want readers to know at all. What they really want readers to know is:

- I struggle with death every day of my life, and that fact bothers me deeply.

- I often feel powerless when confronted with illnesses such as cancer and Alzheimer's.

- What if I fail? What then?

We all start out pretty much the same. We spend nine months in the womb (give or take a few weeks), then come bursting into the world. Sometimes it is a happy event; sometimes not. Nonetheless, we all share those aspects of life. Almost immediately, however, we begin to be differentiated by life's experiences, genetic differences, and our environment.

For some of us, the path is charted before we are born. Our parents have high hopes for us. "He will be a lawyer," or "She will be the first female President of the United States." Parents sometimes think they know what our path is even before we are out of the womb and into the world.

Surprise, surprise! For many of us, there is no chance we are going to get on that path and move forward along the road map our parents (or grandparents) envision for us. Instead, hard as they try, we cannot do that. We may try to please them at first but find we cannot follow the path our parents envision for us. We try to go down that road, but we look for the first exit ramp.

If this is you (and it certainly was me), then this is the book for you. I, too, grew up in a family where certain expectations were held up for me to achieve. I thought of those expectations as hurdles track athletes must jump over. The problem was, I could never get over them. I quickly learned that by hitting them head on, I could still make it around the track.

What happened? I stopped trying. I realized I wasn't going to make it on THEIR path. I kept trying because I wanted their approval; we all seek the approval of our parents. I knew, deep in my heart, it was not going to happen. Unfortunately, my family didn't come to that realization until many years later.

Discovering Who You Are

To begin to plumb the depths of who you are you need to start by writing the first of what will be many personal essays. These essays not only help you explore who you are, but probably will help bring focus to what you write and most likely will become the core of many chapters in your memoir.

Each of us is a distinct person. Our lives are unique. Even if you did not grow up in a family of circus performers, or spend 20 years taming tigers, you have interesting stories to tell. It is not what happened in your life or to you that makes you a writer. It is your distinctive point of view. Before we start on this first (and hardest) essay about our early years (Exercise #1 at the end of this chapter), let's think about some important points that need to be addressed.

Because the personal essay is a form of nonfiction, the self you bring to your essay should be an honest representation of who you are. We are in fact made of many selves: our happy self, our sad self, our indignant self, our skeptical self, our optimistic self, our worried self, our demanding self, our rascally self and on and on and on. But in truth, if we attempt to bring these selves to every essay that we write, we run the risk of seeming so uncertain, so indecisive, that we merely confuse the reader.

A consistent and engaging personality on the page is often a case of choosing which "self" is speaking in a piece and dialing up the energy on that emotion or point of view. Henry David Thoreau likely had days when *Walden Pond* did not fill him with wonder and inspiration but he knew enough to not share those tedious moments. They were beside the point. Or, to put it another way: Dithering is best left to first drafts, and then carefully edited away.

The goal is not to deceive the reader, to pretend to be someone that you are not, but rather to partially isolate a part of who you are, the "you" that you are today, as you meditate on a subject and sit down to write.

The slogan of the literary journal *Creative Nonfiction* is, "You just can't make this stuff up." This slogan is effective, I believe, because of its double meaning. One meaning is that truth is often stranger than fiction. The second meaning reminds the writer that in nonfiction, you are not just making stuff up.

So, don't fake it. Don't act all pious on the page if you are not, in fact, a devout person. Don't generate false outrage over something you don't care that much about. Don't be a hypocrite. Don't try to project an image because you think it will please people—parents, children, friends. But you can highlight a particular trait, if it is in fact true to your nature, and shine a bright light upon it for a few pages, letting it take center stage.

Look at Robin Hemley's introduction to his essay "No Pleasure But Meanness":

I have a mean bone in my body. In fact, I think I have more than one mean bone. For instance, I hate people who smile all the time. It feels good to say that word, 'hate,' doesn't it? Would you like to try it? Say: 'I hate people who ask rhetorical questions in essays that can't possibly be answered.'

Hemley is being witty here, poking fun at himself and at his overuse of the rhetorical question. He is also signaling the reader that this essay will focus on that part of him that can be called "mean," or critical.

Hemley is a very likable, extremely funny man. Yet he no doubt has his mean moments, times when the things that annoy him lead to testiness or sharp anger. We all have that side to us, I believe. Perhaps inspired by William Hazlitt's, "On the Pleasure of Hating", Hemley is taking a moment in his own essay to explore that aspect of himself, closely and specifically.

The essay continues with the author lodging numerous complaints against folks who smile too much in photographs, against the checkout clerk at Walmart, against his kindergarten teacher—and though Hemley continues to leaven his bread of anger with humor and occasional winks to the reader, he does reveal a part of who he is honestly, clearly and with interest.

Another good example is Joan Didion, who begins her essay "In the Islands" with these two sentences:

I tell you this not as aimless revelation but because I want you to know, as you read me, precisely who I am and where I am and what is on my mind. I want you to understand exactly what you are getting: You are getting a woman who for some time now has felt radically separated from most of the ideas that seem to interest other people.

Well, you simply can't get much clearer, or more honest, than that.

That slight aspect of your personality (or fantasy life, or hidden world) that you think so odd, so peculiar, so weird, that you've kept it a secret your entire life, is most likely far more common than you think. We're all made of similar stuff, we human beings. Even our most closely guarded insecurities are often commonly held, though most individuals keep these parts of themselves so hidden that there's little chance to discover the commonality.

But writers are different. We do share. And along the way readers come to an understanding that we are all very much alike.

The French essayist Michel de Montaigne devotes much of his essay "Of Repentance" to this notion of universality.

Consider these sentences:

Others form man; I only report him: and represent a particular one, ill fashioned enough, and whom, if I had to model him anew, I should certainly make something else than what he is: but that's past recalling. … If the world find fault that I speak too much of myself, I find fault that they do not so much as think of themselves. But is it reason, that being so particular in my way of living, I should pretend to recommend myself to the public knowledge?"

Here, Montaigne is addressing a bit of anticipated criticism. In modern parlance, the criticism might go like this:

Just who the heck do you think you are, Mr. Montaigne, to write about yourself all of the time? Shouldn't you confine your writings to the vaunted geniuses and holy persons of past ages, instead of focusing all of the time on our own unproven self?

He goes on to say (in his now quite-dated syntax):

I have this, at least, according to discipline, that never any man treated of a subject he better understood and knew, than I what I have undertaken, and that in this I am the most understanding man alive: secondly, that never any man penetrated farther into his matter, nor better and more distinctly sifted the parts and sequences of it, nor ever more exactly and fully arrived at the end he proposed to himself. … I speak truth, not so much as I would, but as much as I dare; and I dare a little the more, as I grow older; for, methinks, custom allows to age more liberty of prating, and more indiscretion of talking of a man's self.

Montaigne is answering his critics by asserting:

Oh yeah, well let me tell you this much, buster. What I know best is my own self, and I know my own self really, really well, because I'm willing to study this subject and truly consider it in ways that others have not been willing to do. And if what I find is that I'm not so bloody perfect, well then I'll tell you that. Because I'm too old to waste time and hide behind niceties. I'm looking for the truth.

Montaigne, underneath all the complex sentences and fancy language, is making a simple assertion. It's his belief that if he captures a true portrait of himself, he'll capture something universal, something recognizable to everyone.

Or, as he puts it elsewhere in the same essay: ... *Every man carries the entire form of human condition.*

Memoirist Sue William Silverman often receives letters and e-mails from readers, and recently she shared a fascinating reaction to some of the responses to her first two books, *Because I Remember Terror, Father, I Remember You* and *Love Sick.*

Silverman's memoirs are deeply personal and honest about events and behaviors in the author's past, and many of the notes Silverman finds in her mailbox say, in so many words, "I feel as if I know you." In response to this, Silverman writes:

Both memoirs frequently elicit this response ... even though both books are very different. What does Karen know about me? Marie? Karen knows what it was like for me to grow up in an incestuous family. Marie knows what it was like for me to recover from a sexual addiction. To Karen, the real me is one thing; to Marie, the real me is something, someone different. Even so, does this mean that all I am—as a writer and as a woman—is an incest survivor/sex addict? Is that it?

I can only relate to your characters in the narrative of your memoir through you. I cannot see them except through your eyes; only you can tell me what they sounded like, how they smelled, how they walked and lived. It is your description that will bring them to life for me and for your readers.

It is important, then, to paint me a picture using your words. This sounds obvious, but sometimes doing it is harder than we expect. Here are some examples of well-rounded descriptions:

From *Harry Potter and the Philosopher's Stone* by J. K. Rowling:

He was a big, beefy man with hardly any neck, although he did have a very large mustache. Mrs. Dursley was thin and blonde and had nearly twice the usual amount of neck, which came in very useful as she spent so much of her time craning over garden fences, spying on the neighbors.

A giant of a man was standing in the doorway. His face was almost completely hidden by a long, shaggy mane of hair and a wild, tangled beard, but you could make out his eyes, glinting like black beetles under all the hair.

From *I Know Why the Caged Bird Sings* by Maya Angelou:

Where I was big, elbowy and grating, he was small, graceful and smooth. ...he was lauded for his velvet-black skin. His hair fell down in black curls, and my head was covered with black steel wool. And yet he loved me.

Her skin was a rich black that would have peeled like a plum if snagged, but then no one would have thought of getting close enough to Mrs. Flowers to ruffle her dress, let along snag her skin. She didn't encourage familiarity. She wore gloves too.

Now that you have given some thought as to what you want people to know about you, let's begin helping your memories by doing a set of worksheets and more exercises.

Remembering Your Mother

What was your mother's name and how old was she when you were born?	
Where did she grow up?	
Did your mother have brothers and sisters? If so, how many and how did they get along?	
Did she work? If so, what did she do?	
What level of education did she attain? What did she study?	
Did your mother have any hobbies? Did she do volunteer work?	
What is your fondest memory of your mother?	
What is your worst memory of your mother?	

Remembering Your Father

What was your father's name and how old was he when you were born?	
Where did he grow up?	
Did your father have brothers and sisters? If so, how many and how did they get along?	
Did he work? If so, what did he do?	
What level of education did he attain? What did he study?	
Did your father have any hobbies? Did he do volunteer work?	
What is your fondest memory of your father?	
What is your worst memory of your father?	

The Relationship Between Your Parents

Special Circumstances:	
Were you a stepchild?	
Were you adopted?	
How did you feel about the world you grew up in and your role in that world?	
Did you feel loved, cared for, and encouraged growing up?	
As a child, did you have a sense of destiny? How old were you?	
Did you have a feeling that you already knew what you were going to be doing when you grew up?	
Describe your family's economic circumstances. Were you more or less well-off than members of your extended family?	

Your Immediate and Extended Family

List the people who lived in your house—siblings (brothers and sisters), cousins, or and other adults or children to whom you were close.	
Your extended family— uncles, aunts, cousins, or anyone who was an important part of your childhood. You don't need to list every extended family member, but it is good to know those family members who paid an important role in your childhood.	
What was your parent's upbringing? Did they ever talk about it or was it a subject that was not discussed?	
Did your parent's lives turn out as they expected? If not, what did they aspire to accomplish as adults?	

Think about your brothers and sisters. Were they pests, always bothering or teasing you? Or, were they loving companions?	
If you were an only child, did you long to have brothers and sisters in your household? Or, were you glad to be alone?	
How did you celebrate holidays or special events?	
Did religion play a part in your upbringing?	

Your Grandparents

If one or more of your grandparents died before you were born, what did your family tell you about them? How did your family describe those grandparents to you? Such things as education, personality, and work.	
For your grandparents who were alive while you were growing up, brainstorm and write as much as you remember about each grandparent. Try to capture as many memories as you can.	
What were the stories of each of your grandparent's lives?	
Were they active in your life?	
Did you like your grandparents?	

Other Extended Family Members Who Played a Positive Role in Your Life

Sometimes neighbors, religious leaders, or other people in your community had a big influence on you as a youngster. Maybe it was a Little League coach, a music instructor, or a dance teacher. Make a list of those people. When you have finished, draw a circle around one of the names.

Name of the person who influenced me	Their role in my life	Their influence on me

Whose name did you circle on the previous page? Did you pick that person because they helped you the most, had a positive influence on you, and helped to make you the person you are today? You need to explore and understand the important role he or she played in forming or molding you as you moved through various stages of your life.

Answer each of the questions about that person using the prompts in the following worksheet.

What was their role in your life? Caregiver? Religious instructor? Disciplinarian?	
Did he or she write you letters of encouragement?	
Did you want to be like them when you grew up?	
What was his or her influence on you? What did they hope for or expect from you? Did they expect straight "As" or did they expect you to be creative, happy, and a free spirit?	
What talent did they have?	
Did they participate in holiday rituals? Was he or she always there for the holidays? Did he or she send you special gifts on your birthday?	

Essays

Writing an essay is an excellent opportunity for you to give details to events in your childhood. Here are seven essay assignments about your childhood that will help when you are ready pick the theme for your memoir. Try to keep each essay under seven pages.

1. Write an essay about the first 10 years of your life. What are your memories? What made you happy? What made you sad?

2. Write two essays; one about your father and one about your mother. In constructing your essays, think about their backgrounds, their education, their temperament, how each interacted with you, and how each influenced you.

3. Write essays about your siblings. Think about how you interacted with them and how they influenced you. Were you rivals or was there more of a comradely, even loving, relationship between you and your brothers and sisters?

4. Write an essay about your earliest memories up to the age of nine or ten. When you are a child your life usually centers around your immediate and extended family. As you explore your early memories think of who played a fundamental role in shaping you. Much of what and who you are today, began in that period of time, so give careful thought to deep feelings and memories.

5. Write an essay about the person who played an important role in making you the person you are today.

6. Pick one year in the first 12 years of your life and write a story about that year and why it is so important. What experience or event occurred during that year to make it so important and how has it affected your life?

7. Usually, at some point in our teen years, something embarrassing happens to us that we still remember vividly. Take a moment and think about those embarrassing moments, pick one, and write an essay about what happened.

Chapter 3 - Step 2

Types of Memoirs

Now that you have an idea of what a memoir is and how it differs from biographies and autobiographies, let's turn our attention to the basic types of memoirs.

You will need to decide about the type of memoir you want to write. There are six basic types of memoirs. They do not exist in isolation. Your memoir probably will fall into one over-arching type, such as *Family History*, but it may include parts of other types such as *Overcoming Adversity* as well as *Spiritual Guide*.

Once you select, your choice is tentative. As you write, recall, and think, your ideas will change and you may decide you do not want to write a *Family History* memoir, you want to write an *Overcoming Adversity* memoir. That is fine. Nothing is set in concrete until your memoir is printed. Part of the creative process is being flexible and being willing to change at any point in the process of creating your memoir. Indeed, all authors write, rewrite, edit, revise, and then write some more.

So, let's take a look at the most common types of memoirs:

Family History

In *Family History* mode, we are relating to our lineage and the stories associated with it. Many people who do research into their heritage or ancestry write this type of memoir. In the *Family History* mode, you need to remember:

- You will be in the memoir, but you may not be the central character (unless your ancestors had some important bearing on your life). Therefore, you will need a lot of character development dealing with family members. As a result, you may need to do some research into the family to get your facts straight.

- Try to avoid turning your writing into a drawn out non-story of the lives of others rather than your story. It is critical that you pick a message or theme at the outset as to why you are writing in the *Family History* mode.

The problem with *Family History* mode is twofold:

1. You often are not the central character (unless your ancestors had some important bearing on your life).

2. It can become a boring, drawn out non-story of the lives of others rather than your story.

So, if Great-granddad was a drinker, and Granddaddy was a drinker, and Daddy was a drinker, and you were a drinker but overcame it, then it does have something to do with you. Or maybe the drinking affected you as a child, and therefore you decided from an early age to never drink.

If you are using *Family History* as your model, make certain the stories you are telling had an effect on you. Otherwise, it belongs in *Biography*.

Spiritual Guide

If you think of your life as a journey without a road map or GPS, and somehow you got lost along the way, then perhaps *Spiritual Guide* is for you IF:

- You were hopelessly lost.

- You had abandoned all hope.

- Someone or something (a Higher Power, God, the Universe, Buddha, another person in the form of a teacher or religious person, etc.) helped you find your way.

If this happened to you, then telling your story from the viewpoint of starting out, getting lost, and finding your footing through the help of someone or something else, then this is a good model for you. I am not referring to those people whose parents insisted they should be a doctor or astronaut when the person wanted to be a writer.

If you had abandoned all hope and want to write this type of memoir, there are several things to keep in mind:

- It is important to be brutally honest. No sugar coating. No half way here.

You were LOST—got it? You had reached the end of the line. Suicidal (well, maybe not quite that bad, but you had considered it).

- You are willing to admit that you had no power over your situation. (Read the Alcoholics Anonymous Ten Step Pledge).

- Someone or something other than you (because you were powerless) pulled you from the abyss and put you back on the path.

- The new path was not easy; maybe you slid off. But in the end, you became the person you are today because of that "something" else.

This type of memoir can be a brutal, empowering, uplifting memoir. It does not have to start from the day you were born. It can be an episode (my wife left me, my dog ran away, my truck got repossessed—any good country western song should give you some idea). But be careful, it can become preachy and melodramatic.

And no one wants to hear that!

Path to Enlightenment

In the *Path to Enlightenment,* you figure out what is needed to change your life and, through a series of experiences, you make the changes. It is a do-it-yourself version of the *Spiritual Guide* track.

In Buddhism, it is called the eightfold track. So, the eight pursuits in seeking enlightenment are:

1. Understanding

2. Motives

3. Speech

4. Action

5. Means of livelihood

6. Effort

7. Intellectual activity

8. Contemplation

In brief, the eight elements of the path are:

1. Correct view, an accurate understanding of the nature of things, specifically the *four noble truths,*

2. Correct intention, avoiding thoughts of attachment, hatred, and harmful intent,

3. Correct speech, refraining from verbal misdeeds such as lying, divisive speech, harsh speech, and senseless speech,

4. Correct action, refraining from physical misdeeds such as killing, stealing, and sexual misconduct,

5. Correct livelihood, avoiding trades that directly or indirectly harm others, such as selling slaves, weapons, animals for slaughter, intoxicants, or poisons,

6. Correct effort, abandoning negative states of mind that have already arisen, preventing negative states that have yet to arise, and sustaining positive states that have already arisen,

7. Correct mindfulness, awareness of body, feelings, thought, and phenomena (the constituents of the existing world), and

8. Correct concentration, single-mindedness.

In the Christian religion, it often involves forgiveness. Many of us have had that experience where we had to forgive someone who wronged us before we could move on. Someone summed it up by saying, "Enlightenment is when you stop reading fortune cookies."

What I Did and What I Would Do Differently (WIDAWHIWDD)

We could call this the advice column mode, or the cycle version, or the "repeat it until you get it right" version.

If you have a particular experience that is a watershed moment in your life, this may be the best vehicle for you. In the *WIDAWIWDD* model, the author talks about a major turning point in the author's life.

Possible structure:

- My father was an alcoholic. He beat my mother.

- I swore I would never marry a drinker.

- I married a closet drinker who did the same thing to me my father did to my mother.

- I got a divorce.

- I met another man.

- I married him.

- Repeat 3 and 4.

- Introspection: why was I choosing the same type of person?

- What I did to change it.

- How to avoid it again.

You have to be candid. You must accept blame for your contribution to such a relationship, explain how you came through it and came out on the other side.

Coming of Age

There are so many possibilities that arise from the *Coming of Age* memoir. They could include:

- A child trying to understand his or her parents.

- Growing up in a Japanese internment camp during WW II.

- Being abandoned.

- Being adopted and searching for birth parents.

- Living with a mentally ill sibling.

The variations are endless. Many (but not all) *Coming of Age* stories are written in the child's voice in the present tense. Telling this type of story in this way (through a child's eyes) adds a different dimension to the memoir.

An adult would probably tell a completely different version because of their life experiences added to the narrative. A child, however, doesn't have that advantage of life experience, so the tale is quite different.

The advantage of these two observations (adult versus child) brings us to a vantage point. When you write a memoir (whether it is *Coming of Age* or one of the other types) you should practice thinking of your work from two vantage points:

Writer's Coma:

Here you are remembering your experience and shaping it into an interesting narrative. Your mind slips into the time frame of the story, giving the reader the unique power of your circumstances, environment, thoughts and reactions. Your reaction to the situation is unique to you.

Reader's Point of View:

When readers begin to delve into a book, they want to know more about the journey it will take them on. That is why the first few paragraphs of a book are so important. We call it the hook. If you don't "hook" them in the introduction or first chapter, you will lose them and they won't want to continue reading.

Overcoming Adversity

The last major type of memoir is the *Overcoming Adversity* mode. The mode can also be characterized as the *Inspirational* mode because part of your motivation for writing is to impart the lessons you learned as well as to inspire.

Subjects often dealt with in this mode are mental illness, alcoholism, a debilitating accident, abuse, and an untimely (sudden) death. As with all memoirs, you must be honest. In this mode, that honesty may be taxing because of the subject matter, but it is vital to the success of the message.

Other Types of Memoirs

Multicultural Memoirs:

These are stories about cultural mixing. Some of us have adapted to life in a different country as immigrants, expatriates, or exiles. If we didn't assimilate personally, we have parents or grandparents who did. Language barriers, dress, and customs from another place are rich stories. When we look at them, they provide insight into the discovery of our true self.

Travel Memoirs:

You may have spent some time in an interesting place learning from the people and places you visited. *Eat, Pray, Love* by Elizabeth Gilbert falls into this genre as does *Under the Tuscan Sun* by Frances Mays, *Wild: From Lost to Found on the Pacific Crest Trail* by Cheryl Strayed, *The Good Girl's Guide to Getting Lost: A Memoir of Three Continents, Two Friends, and One Unexpected Adventure* by Rachel Friedman.

Near Death Experience:

Heaven is hot these days. Books like Todd Burpo's *Heaven is for Real* have been off the charts for years. Make sure you can back up your claim that you died. People who read these stories can spot a phony a mile away.

The O.M.G. Memoir:

The *Oh My God* memoir is usually about someone who had an unusually hard life, maybe a nomadic, poor, often empty belly, hardscrabble life. Our protagonist (you) escapes her or his poverty, eventually moves to some place like New York City where after hard work and dedication he or she becomes successful. One night, on the way to a party, sitting comfortably in the cab that just picked you up, you see a woman digging through the dumpster. It's your mother! *OMG*! What to do! To find out, read *The Glass Castle* by Jeannette Wells.

Now, it is time for you to think seriously about what type of memoir you will be writing. The worksheets and exercises on the next few pages should help you home in on what category your work is best suited for.

To Help You Decide the Type of Memoir You Want to Write:

1. Make a list of the goals, dreams, and aspirations you had from the time you entered school until the time you left or graduated.

2. Divide the list into time periods such as when you were in elementary school, when you were in junior high and high school, and when you went off to college or got your first real job.

3. Now, look at the above list and make a note of how your goals, dreams, and aspirations changed as you grew and developed.

4. What life changing events occurred before you were 18 and how did that event (or events) change your goals and aspirations?

5. What were your hopes and dreams before the age of 18?

Worksheet #2

1. Go back and review the types of memoirs in this chapter. Make a list of them in descending order of importance in terms of what you see yourself writing.

2. Go back over the list you have just made and see if there is a type of memoir you are fairly sure you can eliminate. Also look at the list and see how you might include types of memoirs as sub portions of the overall main thrust of your memoir.

ॐ

Now that you have completed the worksheets, let's write two essays from two viewpoints:

Essay One: Hopes and Dreams

You listed your hopes and dreams before the age of 18 on one of your worksheets. Now go over that list and write an essay of how you made strides toward fulfilling your goals, dreams, and aspirations or how they changed as you grew and developed.

*   What were your main life achievements during those early years?

*   Did others support your aspirations or did you have to rely on yourself primarily?

Essay Two: How I See Myself

We all face challenges at one time or another. Many of those challenges come in the first 18 years of our lives. Sometimes it is a health crisis. Sometimes it is a family crisis.

*   How did your mental, emotional, and physical health affect the life you have lived?

*   During those years did you struggle with your body image? What was that like?

Chapter 4 - Step 3

Deciding the Type of Memoir to Write

Early in the process of writing your memoir you need to begin thinking of two things:

First, what is the message you want the reader to take away, or to put it another way, what is your reason for writing? It is a good idea to spell out this reason in your *Introduction*. Give the reader a heads-up about your purpose. That purpose can be anything from I want my descendants to know about me and their ancestors, to I want to tell my story of overcoming adversity.

Second, what theme or themes are the threads that run through your writing? Themes such as love, forgiveness, abuse, the power of faith and how that faith changed your life, or any theme that amplifies and gives meaning to your purpose for writing.

These two things, your purpose and the themes of your memoir, will help guide you through the writing process. They will help you stay focused. Also, they are not set in stone. As you begin to think about your life more and more memories will come flooding back. These memories may (and probably will) alter and even completely change your purpose for writing and will almost certainly have an impact on your theme(s).

You also need to remember that the types of memoirs do not exist in isolation. We mentioned this earlier, but it is worth repeating: your memoir will contain elements of several memoir types. For example, if you decide to write a *Family History* memoir you will probably have elements of you or a member of your family *Spiritual Guide* or your *Coming of Age*. If you write a *Path to Enlightenment* memoir there is a very good chance that *Overcoming Adversity* will play a pivotal role in your narrative.

Flexibility and Honesty

The two important things to remember in memoir writing are you must be flexible and you must be honest.

- Flexible in your willingness to adapt and change as your memory opens doors long closed and takes you back to times and events you have forgotten. You will need to re-examine your purpose and message periodically.

- Honest in that you may recall some painful aspects of your life, events and interaction with people you have blocked out. If you decide to address these aspects of your life, you will need to be candid. As the memories come flooding back, you may need to make changes in your approach to writing.

If you cannot be brutally honest about a subject or event, do not introduce it into your manuscript. If you decide to be coy or spin the topic, the readers will pick up on it and you will lose credibility.

Ask Someone

Writing about ourselves is difficult because none of us sees ourselves objectively. All writing can be intimidating because we intuitively know we are exposing a lot about ourselves just in the act of writing: our knowledge of English, our spelling ability, our ability to be clear and logical on paper, and (rightly or wrongly) our level of education. Now, in addition to those considerations, we are the subjects of our writing.

A place to start is to ask friends and family members to write a few paragraphs of how they saw us at various stages in our lives. Don't get your hopes too high. It is difficult and friends and family are reluctant to say anything even remotely negative. I tried asking friends, and only one responded. Why? Because people are often hard pressed to be honest and tell someone about his or her flaws or weaknesses. It is, nevertheless, worth a try. I tried it and the answer I got was pretty thin gruel, but there were a few insightful nuggets in what I received.

Sensitive Subjects

Every family has problems, and every family has a black sheep or two. So how do you deal with those issues?

You will need to give careful thought to this aspect of your memoir. The people you are writing about may be people you love very much. You need to be honest, tactful, respectful, and understanding in dealing with individuals with problems. In my memoir, I had to tackle the mental illness and alcoholism of both my mother and my brother. This was painful but had to be done. It took me a long time, and many drafts, to settle on the words that were honest, but respectful to the people I loved.

One thing you can do as you tackle sensitive subjects is to read the works of other authors who have dealt with these issues and problems. I found *Dime Store* by Lee Smith helpful in dealing with one's heritage, mental illness, and the loss of a child.

Not Sure? Start with This

If you are not sure what type of memoir to write or how to begin, try starting with the *Family History* template. This category is probably the broadest of all memoirs and will give you a platform to start exploring your life and the history of your interaction with your relatives.

Exercises for Chapter 4

Worksheet #1 Message and Type of Memoir

Now that you have thought (and written) about the people who played an important role in your life, think about the type of memoir you would like to write. At this stage in the creation and writing of your memoir what is the one message you want people to take away from your words? To do this, write one sentence that captures the main point of why you are writing.

Once you have decided the main message you want the reader to take away from your memoir, make a tentative decision about which type of memoir you will write. The answer to both this question and the first question can change (and probably will). You will find as you begin to plumb the depths of your memories more and more things will occur and both your main message and the type of memoir is likely to be altered or changed.

What themes do you envision running through your memoir? Make a list of possible themes that could become the main theme of your memoir.

Worksheet #2 Conceptualizing the Project

Once you have finished Worksheet #1, try to envision how your memoir will proceed, how it will be developed. In order to do this, write a rough, detailed outline of how you see your memoir developing.

Once the outline is done, go back and look at it with the idea of breaking the outline into chapters. Then write a proposed chapter outline of the memoir, complete with titles for each chapter. This process will both help you formulate your story and make sure there is logic to the sequencing of what you are writing.

൞

Now that you have given serious thought about the type of memoir you would like to write. Let's begin putting down on paper some essays that will play a role in most any memoir.

Essay One: My Family and Me

Everyone has a family. It may be your birth family (biological), or an extended family. Perhaps you were a foster child who created your own family later when you chose a partner to share your life. Whatever the family structure, we want to know about it. Now, write a short story (approximately six pages) about what it was like to grow up in your household. In this story also include one family member who stands out in your mind. Tell us how this person influenced you.

Essay Two: Wealth

Wealth, or the lack of it, is a dominant theme in our lives. How did you view financial security from your childhood through your teenage years into adulthood? Did anything ever threaten your financial security in your pre-adult days? How did that affect your view of money? Did you see it as power, safety, freedom or some other definition?

Chapter 5 - Step 4

Defining Characters

The reader can only relate to your characters in the narrative of your memoir through you. The reader cannot see them except through your eyes; only you can tell me what they sound like, how they smell, how they walk, and how they live. It is your description that will bring them to life for your readers.

It is important, then, to paint a picture using your words. This sounds obvious, but sometimes doing it is harder than we expect. Here are some examples of well-rounded descriptions.

C3✻80

From *Harry Potter and the Sorcerer's Stone* (J.K. Rowlings, Scholastic, 1998):

He was a big, beefy man with hardly any neck, although he did have a very large mustache. Mrs. Dursley was thin and blonde and had nearly twice the usual amount of neck, which came in very useful as she spent so much time craning over garden fences, spying on neighbors. (p. 1)

A giant of a man was standing in the doorway. His face was almost completely hidden by a long, shaggy mane of hair and a wild, tangled beard, but you could make out his eyes, glinting like black beetles under all the hair. (p. 46)

CB✻80

From *I Know Why the Caged Bird Sings* (Maya Angelou, Bantam, 1993):

Where I was big, elbowy and grating, he was small, graceful and smooth. ...he was lauded for his velvet-black skin. His hair fell down in black curls, and my head was covered with black steel wool. And yet he loved me. (p. 17)

Her skin was a rich black that would have peeled like a plum if snagged, but then no one would have thought of getting close enough to Mrs. Flowers to ruffle her dress, let alone snag her skin. She didn't encourage familiarity. She wore gloves too. (p. 78)

ΩΩ

From *The Poisonwood Bible* (Barbara Kingsolver, HarperCollins, 1998):

We wore our best dresses on the outside to make a good impression. Rachel wore her green linen Easter suit she was so vain of, and her long whitish hair pulled off her forehead with a wide pink elastic hairband ... Sitting next to me on the plane, she kept batting her white rabbit eyelashes and adjusting her bright pink hairband, trying to get me to notice she had secretly painted her fingernails bubble-gum pink to match. (p. 15)

ΩΩ

From *Look Homeward, Angel* (Thomas Wolfe, Simon & Schuster, 1995, originally 1929):

My brother Ben's face, thought Eugene, is like a piece of slightly yellow ivory; his high white head is knotted fiercely by his old man's scowl; his mouth is like a knife, his smile the flicker of light across a blade. His face is like a blade, and a knife, and a flicker of light; it is delicate and fierce, and scowls beautifully forever, and when he fastens his hard white fingers and his scowling eyes upon a thing he wants to fix, he sniffs with sharp and private concentration through his long pointed nose ... his hair shines like that of a young boy—it is crinkled and crisp as lettuce. (p. 135)

So, how do we get our characters from one dimensional, boring silhouettes to three dimensional, fabulous characters that live in the minds of readers?

You Guide the Reader

The characters in our stories, songs, poems, and essays embody our writing. They are our words made flesh. Sometimes they even speak for us, carrying much of the burden of plot, theme, mood, idea, and emotion. But they do not exist until we describe them on the page. Until we anchor them with words, they drift, bodiless and ethereal. They weigh nothing; they have no voice. Once we have written the first words—"Belinda Beatrice," perhaps, or "the dark-eyed salesman in the back of the room," or simply "the girl"—our characters begin to take form.

Soon they'll be more than mere names. They'll put on jeans or rubber hip boots, light thin cigarettes or thick cigars; they'll stutter or shout, buy a townhouse on the Upper East Side or a studio in the Village; they'll marry for life or survive a series of happy affairs; they'll beat their children or embrace them. What they become, on the page is up to us.

Your memoir will contain references to a multitude of characters. The following are tips for helping you, the author, bring your characters to life in the reader's mind.

Eleven Pointers for Building Characters

1. Description that relies solely on physical attributes too often turns into what Janet Burroway calls the *All-Points Bulletin*.

   Descriptions that rely solely on physical appearance read something like this: "My father is a tall, middle-aged man of average build. He has green eyes and brown hair and usually wears khakis and Oxford shirts."

   The above description is so mundane, it barely qualifies as an *All-Points Bulletin*. Can you imagine the police searching for this suspect? No identifying marks, no scars or tattoos; nothing to distinguish him. He appears as a cardboard cutout rather than as a living, breathing character. Yes, the details are accurate, but they don't call forth vivid images. We can barely make out this character's form; how can we be expected to remember him?

   When we describe a character, factual information alone is not sufficient, no matter how accurate it might be. The details must appeal to our senses. Phrases that merely label (like tall, middle-aged, and average) bring no clear image to our minds. Since most people form their first impression of someone through visual clues, it makes sense to describe our characters using visual images. Green eyes don't go far enough. Are they pale green or dark green? Even a simple adjective can strengthen a detail. If the adjective also suggests a metaphor—forest green, pea green, or emerald green—the reader not only begins to make associations (positive or negative) but also visualizes in his or her mind's eye the vehicle of the metaphor—forest trees, peas, or glittering gems.

2. The problem with intensifying an image only by adjectives is adjectives encourage clichés.

   It's hard to think of adjective descriptors that haven't been overused: bulging or ropy muscles, clean-cut good looks, frizzy hair. If you use an adjective to describe a physical attribute, make sure the phrase is not only accurate and sensory but fresh. In her short story *Flowering Judas,* Katherine Anne Porter describes Braggioni's singing voice as a "furry, mournful voice" that takes the high notes "in prolonged painful squeal." Often the easiest way to avoid an adjective-based cliché is to free the phrase entirely from its adjective modifier. For example, rather than describing her eyes merely as *hazel,* Emily Dickinson remarked that they were the *color of the sherry the guests leave in the glasses.*

3. Strengthen physical descriptions by making details more specific.

   In our earlier *All-Points Bulletin* example, the description of the father's hair might be improved with a detail such as "a military buzz-cut, prickly to the touch" or "the aging hippie's last chance—a long ponytail striated with gray." Either of these descriptions would paint a stronger picture than the bland phrase brown hair. In the same way, his Oxford shirt could become "a white Oxford button-down that he's steam pleated just minutes before" or "the same style of baby blue Oxford he'd worn since prep school, rolled carelessly at the elbows." These descriptions not only bring forth images, they also suggest the background and the personality of the father.

4. Select physical details carefully, choosing only those that create the strongest, most revealing impression.

   One well-chosen physical trait, item of clothing, or idiosyncratic mannerism can reveal character more effectively than a dozen random images. This applies to characters in non-fiction as well as fiction. When I write about my grandmother, I usually focus on her strong jutting chin—not only because it was her most dominant feature but also because it suggests her stubbornness and determination. When I write about Uncle Leland, I describe the wandering eye that gave him a perpetually distracted look, as if only his body were present. His spirit, it seemed, had already left on some journey he'd glimpsed peripherally, a place the rest of us were unable to see. As you describe real-life characters, zero in on distinguishing characteristics that reveal personality: gnarled, arthritic hands always busy at some task; a habit of covering her mouth each time a giggle rises up, a lopsided swagger as he makes his way to the horse barn; the scent of coconut suntan oil, cigarettes, and leather each time she sashays past your chair.

5. A character's immediate surroundings can provide the backdrop for sensory and significant details that shape the description of the character himself or herself.

   If your character doesn't yet have a job, a hobby, a place to live, or a place to wander, you might need to supply these things. Once your character is situated comfortably, he or she may relax enough to reveal his or her secrets. On the other hand, you might purposely make your character uncomfortable—that is, put him or her in an environment where he or she definitely doesn't fit, just to see how he or she responds. Let's say you've written several descriptions of an elderly woman working in the kitchen, yet she hasn't begun to ripen into the three-dimensional character you know she could become. Try putting her at a gay bar on a Saturday night, or in a tattoo parlor, or (if you're up for a little time travel) at Appomattox, serving her famous buttermilk biscuits to Grant and Lee.

6. In describing a character's surroundings, you don't have to limit yourself to a character's present life.

Early environments shape fictional characters as well as flesh and blood people. In Flaubert's description of Emma Bovary's adolescent years in the convent, he foreshadows the woman she will become, a woman who moves through life in a romantic malaise, dreaming of faraway lands and loves. We learn about Madame Bovary through concrete, sensory descriptions of the place that formed her. In addition, Flaubert describes the book that held her attention during Mass and the images she particularly loved—a sick lamb, a pierced heart.

Living among those white-faced women with their rosaries and copper crosses, never getting away from the stuffy schoolroom atmosphere, she gradually succumbed to the mystic languor exhaled by the perfumes of the altar, the coolness of the holy-water fonts and the radiance of the taper. Instead of following the Mass, she used to gaze at the azure-bordered religious drawings in her book. She loved the sick lamb, the Sacred Heart pierced with sharp arrows, and poor Jesus falling beneath His cross.

7. Characters reveal their inner lives—their preoccupations, values, lifestyles, likes and dislikes, fears and aspirations—by the objects that fill their hands, houses, offices, cars, suitcases, grocery carts, and dreams.

In the opening scene of the film *The Big Chill*, we're introduced to the main characters by watching them unpack the bags they've brought for a weekend trip to a mutual friend's funeral. One character has packed enough pills to stock a drugstore; another has packed a calculator; still another has several packages of condoms. Before a word is spoken—even before we know anyone's name—we catch glimpses of the characters' lives through the objects that define them.

- What items would your character pack for a weekend? Make a list of everything your character would pack: a *Save the Whales* T-shirt; a white cotton nursing bra, size 36D; a breast pump; a can of Mace; Hershey bars.

- What would she use for luggage? A leather valise with a gold monogram on the handle? An old accordion case with decals from every theme park she or he visited? A duffel bag?

8. Description doesn't have to be direct to be effective.

    Techniques abound for describing a character indirectly, for instance, through the objects that fill her world. Create a grocery list for your character—or two or three, depending on who's coming to dinner. Show us the character's credit card bill or the itemized deductions on her income tax forms. Let your character host a garage sale and watch her squirm while neighbors and strangers rifle through her stuff. Which items is she practically giving away? What has she overpriced, secretly hoping no one will buy it? Write your character's *Last Will and Testament.* Which niece gets the Steinway? Who gets the lake cottage—the stepson or the daughter? If your main characters are divorcing, how will they divide their assets? Which one will fight the hardest to keep the dog?

9. To make characters believable to readers, set them in motion.

    The earlier *All-Points Bulletin* description of the father failed not only because the details were mundane and the prose stilted; it also suffered from lack of movement. To enlarge the description, imagine that same father in a particular setting—not just in the house but also sitting in the brown recliner. Then, because setting implies time as well as place, choose a particular time in which to place your character. The time may be bound by the clock (six o'clock, sunrise, early afternoon) or bound only by the father's personal history (after the divorce, the day he lost his job, two weeks before his sixtieth birthday).

    Then set the father in motion. Again, be as specific as possible. "Reading the newspaper" is a start, but it does little more than label a generic activity. In order for readers to enter the fictional dream, the activity must be shown. Often this means breaking all large, generic activity into smaller, more particular parts: "scowling at the Dow Jones averages," perhaps, or "skimming the used-car ads" or "wiping his ink-stained fingers on the monogrammed handkerchief." Besides providing visual images for the reader, specific and representative actions also suggest the personality of the character, his or her habits and desires, and even the emotional life hidden beneath the physical details.

10. Verbs are the foot soldiers of action-based description.

    Well-placed verbs can sharpen almost any physical description of a character. In the following passage from Marilynne Robinson's novel, *Housekeeping,* verbs enliven the description even when the grandmother isn't in motion.

... in the last years she continued to settle and began to shrink. Her mouth bowed forward and her brow sloped back, and her skull shone pink, and speckled within a mere haze of hair, which hovered about her head like the remembered shape of an altered thing. She looked as if the nimbus of humanity were fading away and she were turning monkey. Tendrils grew from her eyebrows and coarse white hairs sprouted on her lip and chin. When she put on an old dress the bosom hung empty and the hem swept to the floor. An old hat fell down over her eyes. Sometimes she put her hand over her mouth and laughed, her eyes closed and her shoulders shaking.

Notice the strong verbs Robinson uses throughout the description. The mouth "bowed" forward; the brow "sloped" back; the hair "hovered," then "fell" down over her eyes. Even when the grandmother's body is at rest, the description pulses with activity. And when the grandmother finally does move—putting a hand over her mouth, closing her eyes, laughing until her shoulders shake—we visualize her in our mind's eye because the actions are concrete and specific. They are what the playwright David Mamet calls "actable actions." Opening a window is an actable action, as is slamming a door. "Coming to terms with himself" or "understanding that he's been wrong all along" are not actable actions. This distinction between non-actable and actable actions echoes our earlier distinction between showing and telling. For the most part, a character's movements must be rendered concretely—that is, shown—before the reader can participate in the fictional dream.

Actable actions are important elements in many fiction and nonfiction scenes that include dialogue. Actable actions should be an important part of your memoir. In some cases, actions, along with environmental clues, are even more important to character development than the words the character speaks. Writers of effective dialogue include pauses, voice inflections, repetitions, gestures, and other details to suggest the psychological and emotional subtext of a scene.

Journalists and other nonfiction writers do the same. Let's say you've just interviewed your cousin about his military service during the Vietnam War. You have a transcript of the interview, based on audio or video recordings, but you also took notes about what else was going on in the room. As you write, include nonverbal clues as well as your cousin's actual words.

• When you asked him about his tour of duty, did he look out the window, light another cigarette, and change the subject?

• Was it a stormy afternoon?

• What song was playing on the radio?

- If his ancient dog was asleep on the cousin's lap, did he stroke the dog as he spoke?

- When the phone rang, did your cousin ignore it or jump up to answer it, looking relieved for the interruption?

Including details such as these will deepen your character description.

11. We don't always have to use concrete, sensory details to describe our characters, and we aren't limited to describing actable actions.

The novels of Milan Kundera use little outward description of characters or their actions. Kundera is more concerned with a character's interior landscape, with what he calls a character's "existential problem," than with sensory description of person or action. In *The Unbearable Lightness of Being,* Thomas's body is not described at all, since the idea of the body does not constitute Thomas's internal dilemma. Teresa's body is described in physical, concrete terms (though not with the degree of detail most novelists would employ) only because her body represents one of her existential preoccupations. For Kundera, a novel is more a meditation on ideas and the private world of the mind than a realistic depiction of characters. Reading Kundera, I always feel that I'm living inside the characters rather than watching them move, bodily, through the world.

With writers like Kundera, we learn about characters through the themes and obsessions of their inner lives, their "existential problems" as depicted primarily through dreams, visions, memories, and thoughts. Memoir writers use this technique to describe what a character appears to be thinking. Or perhaps another character will reveal his or her dreams.

Other writers probe characters' inner lives through what characters see through their eyes. A writer who describes what a character sees also reveals, in part, a character's inner drama. In *The Madness of a Seduced Woman,* Susan Fromberg Schaeffer describes a farm through the eyes of the novel's main character, Agnes, who has just fallen in love and is anticipating her first sexual encounter, which she simultaneously longs for and fears.

… and I saw how the smooth, white curve of the snow as it lay on the ground was like the curve of a woman's body, and I saw how the farm was like the body of a woman which lay down under the sun and under the freezing snow and perpetually and relentlessly produced uncountable swarms of living things, and born with mouths open and cries rising from them into the air, long-boned muzzles opening … as if they would swallow the world whole …

Later in the book, when Agnes's sexual relationship has led to pregnancy, then to a life-threatening abortion, she describes the farm in quite different terms.

It was August, high summer, but there was something definite and curiously insubstantial in the air. ... In the fields near me, the cattle were untroubled, their jaws grinding the last of the grass, their large fat tongues drinking the clear brook water. But there was something in the air, a sad note the weather played upon the instrument of the bone-stretched skin. ... In October, the leaves would be off the trees; the fallen leaves would be beaten flat by heavy rains and the first fall of snow. The bony ledges of the earth would begin to show, the earth's skeleton shedding its unnecessary flesh.

By describing the farm through Agnes's eyes, Schaeffer not only shows us Agnes's inner landscape—her ongoing obsession with sex and pregnancy—but also demonstrates a turning point in Agnes's view of sexuality. In the first pages, which depict a farm in winter, Agnes sees images of beginnings and births. The earth is curved and full like a woman's fleshy body. In the second scene, described as occurring in "high summer," images of death prevail. Agnes's mind jumps ahead to autumn, to dying leaves and heavy rains, a time when the earth, no longer curved in a womanly shape, is little more than a skeleton, having shed the flesh it no longer needs.

Now that we have looked at building characters and some of the ways to bring characters to life in the reader's mind, take time to do the following practice exercises below. Once you have done that move on to Chapter 6 where we examine the protagonist, the antagonist, the mentor, and the foil.

Exercises for Chapter 5

In the Worksheets and Exercises in an earlier chapter, I asked you to look closely at the period of your life from birth to age 12. Now, we turn to your teenage years.

For most of us, the teenage years (junior and senior high school as well as the first years of college or work) were a traumatic time. We were finding ourselves; our hormones were bouncing all over the place. Some of us were famous football players. We peaked early in high school, or we were beauty queens, or whatever. High school was grand for some of us, but for many of us it was terrible. We never suspected it at this state of our lives—unless we had older siblings and heard their horror stories.

Important People: Make a list of the most important people in your life during this time. Include people who had both a positive and negative impact on you.

Name of the person who influenced me	Their role in my life	Their influence on me (+ if positive; - if negative)

Sexuality: Your teen years were a period of change—your sexuality was developing; you were turning into a man or a woman. How did you handle that change? Was it awkward? Did you fall in love? Did you lose your virginity?

Change in my sexuality viewed as a teenager	Positive/ Negative Experience	How I view it as an adult

Gender Identity: Gender identity is a powerful force. The male/female equation is often a balancing act. It can be confusing at times. Take a moment and go beyond your teen years. Over the course of your life, have your ideas about gender changed? Have you noticed a blending of traditional gender roles in your own life? How have your attitudes about sexual identity changed since your teen years?

How I viewed gender identity as a teenager	Did your view change as you grew into adulthood?	How do you view gender identity now?

Essay

Now that you have completed the worksheets, let's write two essays from two viewpoints:

Essay One: Your Teenage Years

Your teenage years were a critical period in your growth and development into an adult. Education was a vital part of that period and growth. Write an essay about a favorite teacher or professor, probably one who influenced you and helped shape you into the adult you turned out to be.

Essay Two: Your Work History

Did you have a job as a teenager? Did your job have a dominant trade or profession that is part of your work history? How did this come about? Where did it lead to? Did you have dreams of doing a particular type of work? Did your parents have an influence on your career choice?

Notes, Thoughts, Ideas:

Chapter 6 - Step 5

Protagonists, Antagonists, Mentors, and Foils

Protagonists

A protagonist is the main character in a novel, memoir, or story that all the action revolves around. In a novel, drama, or any piece of fiction, the protagonist is the hero of the story, the one we are rooting for from the beginning to the end. In your memoir, you are the main character or the protagonist. The reader follows your life, learns about your problems, and knows your feelings and thoughts.

In a novel, a protagonist needs a weakness; in your memoir, you should be honest and expose your weaknesses. We all have weaknesses, so that should not be difficult, what is difficult is admitting those weaknesses. The weakness can be anything, from something that physically makes the protagonist weak, to an event from his or her past that frightens him or her. It can even be a bad quality.

A protagonist loves. In every book, from every genre, the protagonist loves. If they don't actually fall in love then they should show love. Here again, love was part of your life in many different forms—love of your parents, siblings, someone of the opposite sex, or life partner.

Another emotion you, the protagonist of your story, must reveal, at least once is fear. Fear is the most common emotion; it makes us human, and as I've mentioned before, you need to make your characters as real as possible. Revealing your fears exposes yourself in very uncomfortable ways and may be difficult. But it will help you establish a bond of truth and trust with the reader.

Most of all, protagonists struggle. Life is all about struggle. There were conflicts or problems you, the protagonist, had to overcome many times—some great, some small. Maybe it was beating cancer, putting a crumbling marriage back together, finding true love, or saving a friend or family member with severe problems—possibly saving his or her life through your actions. All of us have struggled in one way or another many times. Struggling is part of life; your struggles will play a role in your story.

Antagonist

Your memoir will undoubtedly include one or more antagonists. An antagonist is a person who opposes, competes with, and fights against the main character in a novel or against you in your memoir. Antagonists are usually, but not always, villains. In a novel, they are the ones we are hoping will fall to their demise. We may have the same feelings about the antagonist(s) in your memoir, but many times we grow from our experience with him or her. They cause your problems, sometimes heartache or pain. An antagonist is almost always a part of a memoir that deals with overcoming difficulty—he or she could be a spouse in an abusive marriage, a rival in school or at work, or a very nasty, gun-toting neighbor.

An antagonist is driven to cause conflict on the main character out of pure spite or for a deeper, darker reason and they won't stop until they see the protagonist fall. In a memoir, the trick to dealing with this sort of antagonist is not to appear vindictive. We recommend when you are dealing with such a person in your life to limit, if not practically eliminate, adjectives.

In dealing with any antagonist in your memoir, let the power of your evidence and facts paint the picture of the individual. Avoid anything that smacks of name-calling or retaliation.

Do not forget that an antagonist can be a hero in your memoir. Having said all of the above about an antagonist, the fact is he or she may be a hero—you did not see it at the time, but later that turned out to be the case. For example, maybe he or she pushed you, and at the time you were angry. Maybe he or she fired you from your job and at the time you were angry. Later you saw this person delivering pizza at Dominos and you realized the person was a *schmuck* and decided you weren't going to be one.

Mentors

It is likely that a number of people helped you along the way, guided you, gave you encouragement, or gave you the break you needed to be a success. They are your mentors. We like to think of mentors as guides. They take us by the hand, lead us down the difficult paths or through troubling times in our lives and then leave. Typically, a mentor is not a permanent fixture in our life journey.

Part of your life's story may be that on one or more occasions you were a mentor. You may have given someone a helping hand. Indeed, if your job was a counselor or psychologist, much of your memoir will deal with stories of your mentoring.

So, in your memoir there may be mentors that were crucial to your development, and you in turn may have been a mentor to others.

There are many different types of mentors:

Accompanying

This mentor makes a commitment in a caring way, which involves taking part in the learning process side-by-side with the learner (the memoir writer). These mentors may have worked with you at various stages of your life. Or, you may have played that role at one time or another.

Sowing

These mentors are often confronted with the difficulty of preparing someone before he or she is ready to change. You may have been obstinate or often in trouble as a teen. A mentor may have worked with you and through patience and understanding sowed the seeds of change, change that was necessary for you to turn yourself around. Here again you may have been this type of mentor. You intuitively knew that what you said might not be understood or even accepted at first, but would make sense over the long run and have value to the person being mentored—perhaps putting him on the path to a successful and productive life.

Catalyzing

The catalyzing mentor can play a significant role when change begins to take place and reaches a critical level of pressure. From that point on learning can escalate. Here the mentor chooses to plunge the learner right into change, provoking a different way of thinking, a change in identity, or a reordering of values. The catalyzing mentor in some respects is the outgrowth of the sowing and/or accompanying mentor. It is a characteristic of mentoring at a critical point when a person is changing. Was there a mentor for you at that point in your life? Did you play such a role?

Showing

A showing mentor can make something understandable by using his or her own example to demonstrate a point, a skill, an activity, an experience, or overcoming a problem. If you were a showing mentor, you will tell the reader of your memoir how you used your own experience to help others.

The Foil

There may be one or more persons in your memoir that played the role of a foil in your life. In creative literature, a foil is a character that contrasts with another character (usually the protagonist) in order to highlight particular qualities of the other character. This may be the case in your life. There may have been a person or individuals who at various times in your life had a significant impact on you. In literature, a subplot can be used as a foil to the main plot. In a memoir, this may also be true and is especially true in the case of the "story within the story" motif. The word foil comes from the old practice of packing gems with foil in order to make them shine more brightly.

You can use the technique of having a foil in a memoir, but do not force such a construction because you think it is a neat literary technique. But if there was an individual that played a significant role in your life and who differed dramatically from you or was, on the other hand, extremely similar to you, but with a key difference setting you apart, feel free to use a foil. The concept of a foil is also more widely applied to any comparison that is made to contrast a difference between two things.

Exercises for Chapter 6

Mentors: Make a list of the people you would consider to have been mentors in your life. Decide what type of mentor the individual was—accompanying, sowing, catalyzing, or showing and circle the type. Once that is done, for each mentor, write three examples to illustrate the type mentor he or she was.

Mentor's Name	How this Person Influenced You
accompanying sowing catalyzing showing	1. 2. 3.
accompanying sowing catalyzing showing	1. 2. 3.
accompanying sowing catalyzing showing	1. 2. 3.
accompanying sowing catalyzing showing	1. 2. 3.

Mentor's Name	How this Person Influenced You
accompanying sowing catalyzing showing	1. 2. 3.
accompanying sowing catalyzing showing	1. 2. 3.
accompanying sowing catalyzing showing	1. 2. 3.
accompanying sowing catalyzing showing	1. 2. 3.
accompanying sowing catalyzing showing	1. 2. 3.
accompanying sowing catalyzing showing	1. 2. 3.

Pick a mentor from each type: accompanying, sowing, catalyzing, or showing. Write a paragraph for each describing how the individual influenced and mentored you.

Antagonists: Make a list of the people you would consider to have been antagonists in your life. How did that person influence you? Was it good or bad? Once that is done, write three examples to illustrate the type of influence he or she was.

Antagonist's Name	How this Person Influenced You
The influence was (circle one): Positive Negative	1. 2. 3.
The influence was (circle one): Positive Negative	1. 2. 3.
The influence was (circle one): Positive Negative	1. 2. 3.
The influence was (circle one): Positive Negative	1. 2. 3.
The influence was (circle one): Positive Negative	1. 2. 3.

Antagonist's Name	How this Person Influenced You
The influence was (circle one): Positive Negative	1. 2. 3.
The influence was (circle one): Positive Negative	1. 2. 3.
The influence was (circle one): Positive Negative	1. 2. 3.
The influence was (circle one): Positive Negative	1. 2. 3.
The influence was (circle one): Positive Negative	1. 2. 3.
The influence was (circle one): Positive Negative	1. 2. 3.

Now that you have completed the worksheets, let's write four essays from three viewpoints.

Essay One: Life is a journey

...and for some people the path is clear. For others, wandering off the path provides new challenges or pitfalls. We all have many choices in our childhood years. These events take us into unchartered territory. Maybe it is catastrophic, like the death of a parent. Or perhaps it is realizing you know what career you want to pursue. Was there something that happened to you as a child that changed the direction of your life? Was there a family crisis? Was there an extremely positive event that transformed your childhood? Were their choices you or someone responsible for you made that took you down a road you regretted later? Is there one turning point in your life that stands out?

Essay Two: Religion

It offers hope to some of us. Others shy away from organized religion and follow a spiritual path. Atheists and agnostics add another dimension to the religious debate. Did your earliest religious beliefs follow you from childhood to adulthood? What changed you and how did you evolve? Did you fall away from your beliefs? What happened?

Essay Three: Mentors

In the worksheet for this chapter, I asked you to make a list of the mentors who helped you out along the way. Now, please write an essay about those mentors and the role they played at various stages in your life.

Essay Four: Career

Please write an essay about your career and work experiences. Did you stumble on your career, as I did? Or, did you follow through on your ambitions as a young man or woman?

Notes, Thoughts, Ideas:

Chapter 7 - Step 6

Who is Telling the Story?

Me and Only Me (First Person)

A memoir is your story. Therefore, it is almost always written in first person. Some of you may have been taught in your high school and college writing courses you should never use the pronouns, "I," "my," and "me." That rule may be ok for some forms of writing, but it is not true for memoir writing.

Stop to think, how else are you going to write about yourself and what you did unless you use a sentence such as, "I went to x school" or "My proposals were accepted by the committee."

So, you will undoubtedly write in first person and with the first person point of view. A story is revealed through a narrator (you) who is also explicitly a character within his or her own story. The narrator reveals the plot by referring to this viewpoint with forms of "I" (i.e., the narrator is a person who openly acknowledges his or her own existence) or, when part of a larger group, "we." Frequently, the narrator is the protagonist, whose inner thoughts are expressed to the audience, even if not to any of the other characters.

You, the memoir writer, are a conscious narrator, as a human participant of past events, an incomplete witness by definition, unable to fully see and comprehend events in their entirety as they unfurl, not necessarily objective in your inner thoughts or sharing them fully, and furthermore may be pursuing some hidden agenda.

Multi-Level Narrative (First Person, Plus)

According to Kori Morgan, *The Pad & Pen*, multi-level narrative "…describes a type of story that follows several protagonists rather than focusing on one main character. In some cases, writers choose this structure to show the individual perspectives of characters in a larger "macro story" and how they relate to each other. In other stories, the purpose is to use the multiple characters' perspectives to establish a larger theme. Knowing the conventions of a multiple narrative can help you identify its use in film and literature, as well as gain ideas for writing projects featuring this structure."

For memoir writers, it can be a useful tool in putting your story or the point you are making into better perspective by having another narrative that compares or contrasts with you.

Multi-level memoirs are typically only *Family History* memoirs. You may have one or more family members whose story you detail as part of the interaction with you and your development.

Types of Multi-Level Narratives

In your memoir, you might want to have several stories exist side by side within a chapter. For example, your marriage and starting a family while at the same time telling the story of the degeneration of your birth family—your mother and brother destroying each other because of mental illness and alcoholism. This is called a tandem multi-level narrative.

Or, you may want to tell a story of separation. You were sent to fight in Vietnam, which is a compelling story in itself, juxtaposed to your young wife and child being left to carry on at home and survive on the pay of an army private.

Your memoir may be a sequential multi-level narrative. Characters in your life may come and go. When they appear, the story becomes multi-level as you explore the character in a variety of ways and go into his or her interaction and impact on you. Once the character is no longer in your life, your memoir moves on. Later a new, significant character will appear and your book takes on a multi-level narrative again.

Characterization

In a traditional memoir, the readers are never far removed from you the person who is telling his or her story. In a multi-level memoir, with each character heading up his or her storyline, development occurs not only through the players' encounters with each other, but through the rich description of each character.

Just as in the case of you, the protagonist in your memoir, the other important characters are revealed on a variety of levels in order to compare and contrast with you. You can delve into others' motivations and backgrounds, as well as similarities and differences between them and you. This multi-level characterization gives your memoir vivid detail, as well as depth. And in turn, the reader will have a better understanding of you.

Theme

If you remember, earlier in this book, I urged you to concentrate on a theme or collection of themes that would be the dominant recurring theme of your writing.

The themes of a multi-narrative memoir are directly tied to the characters. Sometimes the theme can explore how character(s) deal with a particular issue(s). For example, you may be writing an *Overcoming Adversity* memoir. If so, you then will be dealing with problems and setbacks. An underlying theme may be your strength of character or where and how you found the will and inspiration to overcome adversity.

Challenges

A problem with multiple narrative memoirs is they often devote too much attention to too many characters. The desire to link too many stories together can result in characters that are underdeveloped or unnecessary. Remember a memoir is creative non-fiction, so you want to select and accent characters (in addition to the protagonist) who expand, develop, or enrich the point or theme of your memoir. You are not writing an autobiography that marches through all your life in lock step and in minute detail. The theme(s) of your memoir can get lost in a forest of interesting, but not essential characters. Effective multi-level memoirs include a limited number of unique and interesting characters (and their stories) that complement the overall theme.

Multi-narrative memoirs can be complicated, so be careful if you go this route—multi-level narratives require the reader to pay close attention in order not to get lost. That is true in literature. I had to slowly read Joseph Conrad's *Heart of Darkness*, which has a double framework: an unidentified "I" (first person singular) narrator relates a boating trip during which another character, Marlow, uses first person to tell a story that comprises the majority of the work. Within this nested story, it is mentioned that another character, Kurz, told Marlow a lengthy story; however, its content is not revealed to readers. Thus, there is an "I" narrator introducing a storyteller "he" (Marlow), who talks about himself as "I" and introduces another storyteller as "he" (Kurz), who in turn presumably told his story from the perspective of "I."

Second Person (Someone Else)

In the second-person point of view, the narrator refers to at least one character directly as "you," suggesting that the audience is a character within the story. This is perhaps the most common type of narrative point of view for song lyrics (the song being directed towards a particular listener emotionally connected with the narrator) and certain types of poetry, though it is quite rarely found in novels or short stories. In some cases, a narrator uses the second person, to refer to herself or himself.

An author addressing the reader directly is a technique used by, and made popular by, Shakespeare. If you accept my premise that a memoir is best written in a conversational tone so that the reader feels he or she is being talked to directly, then you are doing just that. At some point, you may want your words to address the reader directly, just as the dwarf does in the book and film version of Catherine Ann Porter's *Ship of Fools*.

Unreliable Narrator Voice

Unreliable narrative voice involves the use of a dubious or untrustworthy narrator. This mode may be employed to give the audience a deliberate sense of disbelief in the story or a level of suspicion or mystery as to what information is meant to be true and what is to be false. This lack of reliability is often developed by the author to demonstrate that the narrator is in some state of psychosis. The narrator of Poe's *Tell-Tale Heart*, for example, is significantly biased, unknowledgeable, ignorant, childish, or is perhaps purposefully trying to deceive the audience. Unreliable narrators are usually first-person narrators; however, when a third-person narrator is considered unreliable for any reason, their viewpoint may be termed "third-person subjective."

Naïve Narrator

A naïve narrator can be a buffoon, a fool, or anyone who is incurably naïve. He or she is one who is so ignorant and inexperienced that he or she actually exposes the faults and issues of her or his world. You may have had one or more of these individuals in your life. If you decide to include him or her in your memoir, do it collectively. They are often humorous, but use them sparingly. The humor or idiocy can undercut the message or theme of your memoir.

Naïve narrators are most often used particularly in satire, whereby the user can draw more inferences about the narrator's environment than the narrator. Child narrators can also fall under this category.

Exercises for Chapter 7

- Make a list of events in your life that were noteworthy and could be turned into a stand-alone essay.

- Make a list of people who were in your life, and may have played a part in your life, but whom you really disliked.

- Pick a vacation or trip you took at some point in your life and write an essay about it.

- If you have children, list them, and under each name write a few sentences about how you remember them at various stages of their lives. Were they ever problems? What were their successes and failures? How did having children change your life?

- Make a list of people whom you remember vividly from your young adulthood.

- Write a short essay (a few paragraphs) about each of the people you listed in #5.

ርჳჄე

Now that we have discussed the various types of characters that may appear in your memoir, let's do some character development exercises. Think about the characters that you will be writing about.

1. Make a list of characters you expect to write about.

2. Pick one of those characters. Brainstorm all you know or can remember about that person. (Keep your brainstorming notes throughout your writing process and add to them as you begin to write.)

3. Once you have done step two in this process, decide if you are a subordinate or a superior character to this person and explain why. Perhaps he or she was a mentor, or you played a role in guiding the individual's life.

4. Think about why you are in the role you see yourself in.

5. Decide how you feel about that character. Is it a love or hate relationship? Why?

6. Repeat this process for the major characters who appear in your memoir.

7. Think about your life as a young adult. Write an essay about getting your first full time job after leaving school. How did that job shape you? Did you stay with it, or was it the first of many jobs in your work career?

8. Love and marriage were undoubtedly part of your life during this period of time. Write an essay about falling in love, marrying, and building your life with someone else—and having children.

Notes, Thoughts, Ideas:

Chapter 8 - Step 7

Aargh! Do I Have to Use English?*

(The answer to the question above is, "Unfortunately, yes.")

Now that you have decided to write your memoir, you need a few reminders about correct English. Yes, I know almost all of you have a college degree and passed college level English, but that may have been a long time ago. Rules in English are in a near constant state of flux. So, if you want to put your best foot forward in your memoir, let's take some time to review English.

I often tell my classes that anyone who uses English to make his or her living needs to be recertified every five years to use the language correctly. I am half joking, half serious.

You have decided to write your memoir knowing it is a daunting task; you will be exposing a great deal about yourself.

A survival level skill in English is relatively easy to learn, a superficial look at the language leaves the impression that English is simple and logical. Nothing could be further from the truth. English is riddled with contradictions and inconsistencies. The net result is that using English correctly requires more education than any other Western language.

There are three major U.S. government language schools. The Defense Language Institute in Monterey, California; the State Department's Foreign Service Institute, and the CIA Language Institute.

All three rate languages on a scale from 1-5 in order of difficulty—from "5" the most difficult, to "1," the easiest. The scale is based on the ability to use the languages correctly, not simply to gain a survival skill. All three rate English as a "5."

Native English speakers find it hard to believe that English is a "5." After all, we do not attach genders to our nouns (no masculine, no feminine, no neuter), and we don't change vocabulary or word endings depending on whether a man or woman is speaking. How could English possibly be a "5?"

There are many reasons why correct English is so difficult to use:

1. A rule is not a rule in English; a rule is a suggestion and a place to start. Many of our rules have nearly as many exceptions as they have adherents. I recently read a book by an English scholar who described English grammar and punctuation as three-quarter rules and one-quarter common sense. That is a heck of a way to run a language.

   By the way, if anyone reading this has a child in school struggling with English, the best thing you can do is enroll him or her in one of three foreign languages: German, Latin, or Spanish. All three have rules and abide by them. That is how I learned correct English. I took three years of German in high school and reverse engineered. By drilling on German rules, I came to understand English rules and their exceptions.

2. English is not phonetic; you cannot spell in English based on the sounds of our words. English spelling is probably the most inconsistent and confusing of all the major European languages. Moreover, in writing we rarely use accent marks, which further complicates the problem. At least in French, which is also non-phonetic, accent marks are used in writing to help the reader.

3. There are eight basic parts of English according to grammarians, and one of those, prepositions, is one-hundred-percent idiomatic—there are no rules! We make it more complicated by using prepositions to change the meaning of our sentences. The following three sentences are identical except for the prepositions. Notice how the preposition nudges the reader's expectations about what is to follow:

   --I work in an office.

   --I work at an office.

   --I work for an office.

4. English is the fastest changing major language in the world. Unlike other languages that resist change, English is open to it. For example, the *Academie francaise* has the job of preventing foreign words from being used in French. In fact, it is an offense (legally) if products are sold under their English names. There are many

languages that do not allow borrowing from other languages. This resistance to foreign words most often has to do with the politics of languages more than anything else. Not so English, we borrow freely from other languages and change or modify our rules frequently.

5. English does not have gender-based nouns like most other Western languages. English only has three articles—"the" (the definite article), and "a" and "an" (the indefinite articles). Yet even the use of them is a bit confusing and at times idiomatic. For example, you say, "I am going to the movies," putting the article in front of the noun, but you also say, "I am going to bed," leaving the article out.

❧

How do you know when to use 'a' or 'an?' Simple, right? Not really. The rule or suggestion in English is that if the noun starts with a consonant, use 'a.' If the noun starts with a vowel, use 'an.' So, the following must be a correct English sentence: Ralph has a herb garden. In British English, it is correct, but in American English it is not. The British pronounce the consonant 'h' so they use 'a.' In American English we swallow the 'h' and pronounce the vowel 'e.' So you use 'an.'

The reason for this is based on sounds—on how you pronounce the first letter of the noun. So, in American English, you use 'an' with all vowel sounds except those words starting with a long 'u' or silent 'h.' Are you seated for this one? In speech, according to the *Gregg Reference Manual*, both "a historic occasion" and "an historic occasion" are correct, depending on how you pronounce the word "historic." In written American English, "a historic occasion" is the most common and accepted form. You don't get much more screwed up in the world of languages than having a non-phonetic language with a rule that trumps its other rules, based on sounds!

❧

We need to take a moment and look at the history of English in order to put it into context and to better understand why the language is so difficult to use correctly. English belongs to the broad category of Indo-European languages and traces its origins to around 500 B.C. English language has dramatically changed and altered as invasion after invasion swept over the British Isles.

I know historians and linguists disagree with me, but I consider the foundation of modern English to date from 1066 and the Battle of Hastings, when the French-speaking Normans conquered the Anglo-Saxons. French is arguably the most difficult of the Romance languages; it has difficult grammar, difficult punctuation, and is non-phonetic. The Anglo-Saxon tongue had simpler grammar, simpler punctuation and simple one- and two-syllable words (for the most part). From 1066 on, the mixing begins. What does that mean for modern English? It means that English is a mix of rules and exceptions to those rules, and in English, a rule is really a suggestion.

Thus, in the mixing of the new language, the upper-class words became French as the new rulers imported their language and left the Anglo-Saxon to the swine herders. Most words dealing with sophisticated ideas and thoughts, abstractions, nuances, and innuendos owe their roots to French. The grammar and vocabulary of the common worker remained Anglo-Saxon—simple and to the point.

This means that at the heart of our language, we have two core groups of words, the multi-syllable French-based words, and the one- and two-syllable words of Anglo-Saxon origin. The vocabulary in your memoir should be consistent with the language you use every day. Do not reach for sophisticated, multi-syllable words to try to impress. Believe me, you won't.

CSEO

The study of the English language is very useful for historians, who can trace the rise in power of the Anglo-Saxon nobles by looking at legal English. As the nobles became more powerful they insisted that their vocabulary be inserted into the law. Thus, you have the phenomenon of the double noun in legal English. When you go to your attorney to have your will drawn up, the first sentence may begin as follows:

My last will (Anglo-Saxon) and testament (French for will)……..

The periodic appearance of the Anglo-Saxon nouns alongside French nouns marked a step forward for the Anglo-Saxon nobility and another step forward in the mixing of the two vocabularies.

The willingness to grow and change, then, is an inherent part of modern English. English is receptive to change—particularly American English. Because English is so willing to borrow from other languages and coin new words, English vocabulary is always in flux. This willingness to change gives English a vitality and panache lacking in other languages. It also makes English difficult. Every year a new list of correct American English words appears. As new waves of immigrants come to the United States they bring different foods, different concepts, and different words to describe things. Many of these words become standard American English. The impact of Spanish on American English is already apparent and will continue.

You may say the above is interesting and will give you some answers when you play *Trivial Pursuit*, but what does it have to do with writing a memoir? Well, it underscores the difficulty of the problem writers face—that is making our work as correct as it possibly can be, and keeping up with the changes in English.

Failure to understand the basic writing principles, as well as the variations on those principles, can and does lead to misunderstandings and confusion. One of the basic differences centers on the use of active voice versus passive voice. There seems to be an epidemic of passive voice sentences in some writing circles, coupled with a dearth of active voice sentences.

The decision to use active or passive voice may well depend on your audience, as well as the theme and goal of your memoir. My feeling is that an *Overcoming Adversity* memoir should rely heavily on active voice sentences that are clear. Why? You are imparting information based on the lessons you have learned. This form of memoir will usually be less nuanced and more direct and to the point.

I am not saying don't use passive voice sentences; by all means do use them. Just make sure your memoir is sprinkled with a healthy number of active voice sentences to add clarity. And, for those of you with an attachment to the passive voice, let's take a look at reasons to use it, and be clear when, where, and why it is appropriate. Use a passive-voice sentence:

- When you don't know who the actor is—that is just common sense.

- When you want to emphasize something other than the actor. For example: A bumper crop of wheat was grown by the Russians. (There had been a drought for the last 10 years.)

- When you are making an argument by looking at alternatives and engaging in a dialog with the reader. (The passive voice allows them greater argumentation and interpretation and will show the aspects of the problem you have examined.)

- When you intentionally want to obscure the actor. This type of passive construction is the lifeblood of politicians, who during elections want to give the impression they are coming clean with the electorate. For example: "Mistakes were made!" Yes! By whom? Tell us so we can vote the culprits out of office.

Before I end this grammar and punctuation review, I need to look at the areas where the most errors are made. I have found mistakes writers make center on four parts of English.

Verbs: All aspects ranging from tenses, through verb selection, and subject verb agreement.

Prepositions: English, unlike most other languages, uses prepositions to change the meaning of sentences. And, English complicates the problem because prepositions are one hundred percent idiomatic—there are no rules.

Pronouns: Minimize the use of pronouns. Some advocate extensive use of pronouns as a way of adding variety, and it does. But, with that variety comes the danger of ambiguity. What or who does the pronoun refer to? If you use a pronoun make sure that the antecedent of the pronoun is clear. The pronouns "this, that, these, and those" are frowned upon. They are the demonstrative pronouns and English language purists consider them to be crutches. For example, if you begin a topic sentence with "This means ...," what or who does the "this" refer to? If you use the demonstrative pronouns make sure you identify the reference to "this decision…" or "that rule change …."

CRBO

Sentence structure and grammar can cause problems. Just remember to try and sprinkle your text with a number of short declarative sentences with no internal punctuation. Short sentences pick up the pace of the work. Longer sentences can be a problem because of the internal punctuation, particularly commas. So, be careful of commas. English has over 300 rules for commas. Furthermore, an English sentence can be correct with or without a comma. For example:

I hereby leave all my earthly belongings to the first of my children who lives a good life. Message: The first of my eleven off-spring to shape up and live a good life gets the loot.

I hereby leave all my earthly belongings to the first of my children, who lives a good life. Message: I am leaving the family fortune to my first born because I am rewarding the child for living a good life.

Before I leave commas, I have to mention a student I had not too long ago in class. He had just graduated from a major university and one of his professors had told him not to worry about commas because they are becoming passé and soon will disappear from English. "No!" I wanted to say, "What university did you go to? I want to advise every young person I know to stay away from that school."

Commas are of paramount importance to understanding written English. Look at the difference a comma makes in the following sentences:

1. Ralph quit, saying he was fed up with office politics.

2. Ralph quit saying he was fed up with office politics.

So, English sentences can be correct with or without a comma, and the difference can be significant. Forewarned is forearmed.

⚖

English is a major tool of a writer's trade. The message you send when your work is riddled with errors or is confusing is that you are sloppy, uneducated, and careless, and pay no attention to detail. Why should anyone believe you if your memoir is confusing and error-ridden?

One other thing before moving on; here are five of the recent changes in correct standard English usage:

You now only put one space at the end of a sentence following the punctuation.

It is correct to split an infinitive. When the TV series *Star Trek* came out in the 1960s, its famous phrase to boldly go was incorrect English because it split the infinitive of the verb to go.

It is correct to end a sentence with a preposition, if the alternative construction would be confusing or convoluted.

A one-sentence paragraph is correct in all forms of writing.

It is correct to change verb tenses in a sentence if you have a reason.

Enough. I think I have made the point sufficiently about using correct English.

Exercises for Chapter 8

Before you begin drafting your memoir in earnest:

I suggest you write a few more essays in order to help you collect and organize your thoughts. Here is a list of essays you may find valuable when it comes to putting your memoir together:

Write an overarching essay about your mother. Pick a theme(s) that typifies her as a woman and mother, e.g. nurturing, loving, strong, educated, confident, or supportive.

Write an overarching essay about your father. Just as in the case of your mother, pick a theme(s) that characterizes him or captures him, e.g. honest, faithful, role model, caring, confident, opinionated, or any of the themes listed about your mother.

Write an essay about each of your siblings. Try to capture the essence of your relationship with him or her.

Write an essay about your work and the jobs you held. Were you a housewife or a househusband? Some of the points you might touch upon are, did you find your work rewarding, did you meet your goals and ambitions?

Preparing to write your memoir:

Every writer suffers from writers' block. It is endemic to all of us. So, to begin the process of writing your memoir, begin by writing a series of essays. (And, if possible, have someone review them and give you critical feedback. This feedback is important.) These essays do not have to be done in chronological order. Instead they are essays about any part of your life you want to examine. There is a good chance these essays will become central to some of the chapters in your finished work.

Here are some ideas to write about:

What was something you were afraid of as a child?

What was something difficult you had to do as a child?

What was an embarrassing moment that happened to you as a child or young adult?

Who is someone you lost and what are your memories about him or her?

What event helped to shape your outlook on life?

Describe your favorite teacher in school.

Describe your best childhood friend and your relationship with that person.

When you were a child, how did you imagine yourself as an adult?

What are your earliest memories?

What are some of the memories you associate with springtime?

What are your memories about summer, fall, and winter?

What song, book, public leader, clergy member, or person inspired you?

What is your purpose?

I know this exercise may be difficult at this stage in your writing, but by now you should have some idea about your purpose in writing your memoir. In one sentence, write your purpose or goal in recording your life. For example: to tell my children about my life, to explain the hardships I had to overcome, or to write a best-selling, insightful memoir that will inspire others.

---

*This chapter is adapted from Chapter II, *This Beast The English Language, Intelligence and Crime Analysis: Critical Thinking Through Writing.* David Cariens (High Tide Publications, November 13, 2015)

Notes, Thoughts, Ideas:

Chapter 9 - Step 8

Write Your Memoir

It is now time for you to begin serious drafting of your memoir, if you have not already done so. Earlier, I asked you to do three things to begin conceptualizing your memoir:

One: Determine what the main message of your memoir should be. In other words, to conceptualize why you are writing, and to write that purpose or message in one sentence.

Two: Decide the type of memoir you want to write—*Family History, Overcoming Adversity*; or whatever you think.

Three: Draft a proposed chapter outline of your memoir.

Please return to those three exercises and look at them. After completing numerous worksheets and exercises, is your reason (your message) still the same? If not, draft a new statement of purpose. Is the type of memoir you originally thought you wanted to write still the same? Decide whether the answers to the first two are essentially the same as your original answers or have changed. Go over the chapter outline and make whatever changes are necessary.

Cঙৎର

It is always interesting to see what prompts people to write or whatever gives them inspiration and gets the creative juices flowing. For me, it is music. Or, maybe it is just sit down and do it—brainstorm and get the ideas flowing. That works for me.

Here is a checklist to keep in mind as you go through the process of writing your memoir. Ask yourself the following twelve questions as your write and review your manuscript:

Checklist to Review Your Writing	
1. How does your writing fit into your main goal or purpose?	
2. Have you found your voice? Will the reader be able to "hear" you and visualize what you are writing?	
3. Did you begin in an interesting way?	
4. Did you develop ideas by using interesting or important experiences?	
5. Did you include sensory details (things for the reader to hear, see, smell, feel, and taste)?	
6. Can the reader "see" the locations you are describing?	
7. Can the reader tell the time period of the experiences? Are your words bringing the settings to life?	
8. Did you place ideas and details in meaningful order (not necessarily chronological)?	
9. Did you provide the reader with a natural flow and sequence to the story?	
10. Did you use imagination and creativity, but remain true to the facts?	
11. Can the reader understand the purpose of writing about incidents in your life?	
12. Does the ending leave the reader wondering? In other words, do you provide closure?	

A Word of Caution

Think and chose your words carefully. If you are dealing with contentious issues, always be factual and avoid being accusatory.

According to Judith Barrington, in her excellent book, *Writing the Memoir*:

Many writers engaged in writing a memoir worry about being sued. For most, this is a way of focusing their fear of telling the truth. It is a legitimate concern for only a few.

I agree with Barrington and would add, you will know intuitively if you crossed the line. I can speak from experience. Two of my books, both dealing with school shootings, could have led to legal action. Both are factually correct, but I name names of those who made wrong decisions.

Those bad decisions played a role in the shooting rampages at the Appalachian School of Law in January 2002, and Virginia Tech in April 2007. I was not sued because the best defense against legal action is the truth.

I strongly advise you to seek counsel if you have any questions about possible legal action.

Now, Down to Work.

As you write, take time to let the ideas perk and the memories come back. If you reach a block, get away from the draft. If you feel your words do not capture what you want to say, ask someone to read the pages or paragraphs. Tell that person what your goal is, what you want the reader to take away from your words and ask him or her to be honest. This last point is very important. If you are asking him or her to critique you, say something like this, "I am asking you to look at this because I admire your judgment (and writing skills, if appropriate), please be brutally honest. I would rather be embarrassed with you than have the book go to print and really be embarrassed."

Finally, if you can afford it, hire an editor. You want someone who does not know you well, and has played no role in the writing. It is well worth the money.

Ok, that is it. Good luck! I look forward to reading your words.

About The Author

David S. Cariens

David Cariens is a retired CIA political analyst. He wrote finished intelligence for all levels of consumers including the President and members of the intelligence and policymaking communities. Cariens continues to teach intelligence and crime analysis for the U.S. government and abroad.

He served as a member of the Ad-hoc Program Advisory Committee (PAC) relative to the development of the Bachelor of Applied Public Safety (BAPS) - Specialization in Crime and Intelligence Analysis at Seneca College, Toronto, Canada. He teaches at the University of Richmond's Osher Institute and was an adjunct professor at VCU's Homeland Security Department.

Cariens is a victims' rights advocate. He is the author of *A Question of Accountability: The Murder of Angela Dales* -- an examination of the shooting at the Appalachian School of Law in Grundy, Virginia, and *Virginia Tech: Make Sure It Doesn't Get Out*, an analysis of that rampage.

Cariens is a contributing author to the International Association of Law Enforcement Intelligence Agency's textbook, *Criminal Intelligence for the 21st Century*.

He is on the Board of Directors of the *Writers Guild of Virginia*.

Index

Other Books by David Cariens:

Virginia Tech - Make Sure It Doesn't Get Out

A Question of Accountability: The Murder of Angela Dales

Critical Thinking Through Writing: Intelligence and Crime Analysis

A Handbook for Intelligence and Crime Analysis

Intelligence and Crime Terminology A Glossary of Terms and Acronyms

The America We All Want: Protecting Your Community From Gun Violence